A YOUNG MAN'S GUIDE to Failing with Women

JAY WIGGINTON

AuthorHouse™
1663 Liberty Drive
Bloomington, IN 47403
www.authorhouse.com
Phone: 833-262-8899

Because of the dynamic nature of the Internet, any web addresses or links contained in this book may have changed since publication and may no longer be valid. The views expressed in this work are solely those of the author and do not necessarily reflect the views of the publisher, and the publisher hereby disclaims any responsibility for them.

This book is printed on acid-free paper.

ISBN: 978-1-6655-1778-2 (sc)
ISBN: 978-1-6655-1808-6 (e)

Library of Congress Control Number: 2021903935

Print information available on the last page.

Published by AuthorHouse 02/26/2021

author HOUSE®

About the Author

Hello! I am writing this book to share some of my experiences and failures in the dating world in the hopes that you can find some humor and possible life lessons from them. These stories are all true stories (to the best of my memory) I have experienced along my dating journey.

I am currently living in North Carolina but have lived all over the United States. I joined the military at an early age which contributed to me being a nomad. That experience has allowed me to travel the world and fail with women in all kinds of cultures. I am still currently single so I'm sure there will be more failures in the future. I hope you enjoy the stories!

Critically Acclaimed!

"He tries really hard!"

"At least he paid for dinner."

"I was drunk"

"He's a good friend"

THE EARLY YEARS

I think I had a typical childhood. I played sports, beat up my brother, and did ok in school. Something I did not have growing up was exposure to the opposite sex. One of the first memories I have of being interested in women was the "Hit Me Baby, One More Time" song by Brittney Spears. I was glued to the TV when that music video came on. The first memory I have of actually talking to a girl did not go as well as me and Brittney's relationship. Around middle school, I decided I was going to be a male model for a living. I went and took professional photographs and actually got with an agency. This agency booked me on a few little things. One of those things was a mall opening in the area. I was to model the young men's section. I got to pick out about six outfits and just had to walk back and forth in my section. I was given lines to say if any of the CEO type people came and talked to me. For that gig, I was paid by keeping the clothes I wore and a gift bag. In that gift bag was a pen that came in a fancy case. To a middle schooler, this was something special. What kind of pen comes in a case? It must be something great. My newly discovered like of women kicked into my head. With a gift like this, I'm sure that cute girl in my class would fall in love with me and we would get married. The next day in class, I spent the entire morning putting my plan in motion. The plan was to wait until we go to recess, I would be the last person out, I would put the gift bag with the pen on her desk with a note asking if she would go out with me. As was custom in those days, you had to have the "Check Yes or No" option at the bottom of the note. When the bell sounded for recess, I put the plan into action. I acted like I had to tie my shoe while the room cleared. I then placed the bag in her chair so then she would see it, but not the rest of the class. During that recess, I think I probably stared at my future wife and dreamed of our life together. Recess came to an end and I wanted to be the first one back in the room so I could see her reaction and be there for the inevitable hug and kiss that was to follow. I sat down. She made it to her seat and stopped in confusion with a slight smile on her face. She picked up the bag and pulled out the note first followed by the gift of gifts. She was grinning almost ear to ear at this point. Nailed it. She then read the note. The smile began to slowly shrink. I thought it was shock that this was finally happening for her also and she must have gotten lost in the daydream of our future, too. She put the note down to pen her answer, folded up the note, and walked it over to my desk. I open it in excited anticipation. "No". I was given the pen back shortly after.

I WASN'T READY

As you can tell, I have always been awkward with women and that rolled into high school. The year was 2002 and I was a sophomore in high school. I was the Commander of my high school JROTC unit, in the National Honor Society, and wore JNCO jeans. I was not one of the popular kids. My only experience "dating" up until this point was being too scared to talk to my 6th grade crush even though we dated about three weeks. Our entire relationship consisted of me trying to avoid face to face interaction. I would call her in the afternoons, and I would actually write out topics that I wanted to talk about so there would be no awkward silence. When I ran out of topics, I would always make up an excuse to get off the phone. By the grace of the dating gods, I started dating this girl in my second year of high school. I forget how it actually happened, but I'm assuming she lost a bet. After about a week of continuing my dating tradition and trying to avoid her at all costs, she wrote me a note asking why I had not kissed her. There it was. The time had come. I wasn't ready. I remember getting extremely nervous knowing that I had to lose my kissing virginity. At this point, my friends were all making out and I probably made up lies that I was just kissing all the time. This girl did not have to lie about her kissing pedigree. I knew she was experienced which did not ease my nerves at all. The bell rang to switch classes and I stood up out of my desk knowing my life was about to change. When I saw her, I tried to keep it casual on the outside even though my insides were in a million knots. "Keep it cool... You've kissed dozens of girls." After the short walk to my next class, I worked up the courage and went for the kiss... I made a crucial mistake and closed my eyes too early causing me to miss and got left nostril. Embarrassed, I turned and ran into the gym... she broke up with me shortly after.

ANOTHER MILESTONE

As my high school career advanced, I grew more awkward. Another example would be losing my virginity. I had made it to senior year of high school with my virginity intact. I was scheduled to take Spanish class and got lucky when an attractive girl sat right in front of me. Before cell phones, we would communicate with notes, so me and her would just pass notes back and forth all class. (I don't speak a lick of Spanish) Most of the conversation was about her boyfriend and how poorly he had treated her. Ex. "He went out with his friends and didn't invite me.", "He didn't want to go to the flower garden", "All I wanted was a Valentine's present even though I said I didn't want anything". Awful stuff. Of course, my response to most of these notes was how I would never do that to her and she's the greatest thing since sliced bread. One day, she came to class with a pep in her step and sat down to vigorously write me a note (instead of just telling me). The note had said how she had just broken up with the boyfriend. My first thought was "Fuck, I've made a lot of promises here". Anywho, we started dating and her parents were the strict kind that if we wanted to hang out, it had to be in their house, in the living room, with them there. As a relationship novice, I was ok with this. It gave me an excuse to not be suave because her parents were around. After about a month of this, her dad gave us permission to go out on a Friday night as long as we were home by 9pm. I took her to TGIFriday's and I had the chicken fingers. We left dinner around 8pm with plenty of time to get home. I remember thinking how happy her dad was going to be that she was home early. On the way back, she said she wanted to walk around a lake in the area. Initially, I resisted saying we didn't have THAT much time to walk around a lake! On the other hand, this was the first girl to let me touch her butt, so what am I going to say? So we pulled into the park and she told me to park in a children's playground a good ways from the lake. Again, I resisted saying the lake was another half mile away! We were never going to make it around the lake and back in time. (I'm an idiot). We parked and she immediately started kissing me.

I NOW knew what was up. When my body realized what was happening, I must have went into a mild state of shock. I started shaking and feeling nauseous. My only idea of sex up to this point was the 11oclock soft core porn I used to set my alarm for to watch. Nonetheless, there was no turning back. I had a condom in my glove box that had probably been there for 3 years at this point and I pulled it out. I tried to put it on only to realize that it did not go on. After a few attempts, she reached over and flipped it around. This is how I learned condoms only go on one way. She assumed the position on the opposite side of the single cab truck and with my violently shaking arm on the dash, I went to get on top. She was guiding the action while I slumped into position. I think my penis might have grazed her vagina before I immediately started to cum. To make it worse... I didn't know that this was not supposed to happen. I was smitten knowing that I JUST HAD SEX. Her, not so much. Rumor has it you can still hear her disappointment in that parking lot on quiet summer nights.

THE MILITARY YEARS

I joined the military at 17 and joined an infantry unit. This meant I only interacted with guys. During my entire four-year enlistment, I made out with one stripper. That's it. I did still manage to have a couple awkward female interactions. One of them was on my 21st Birthday. I had turned 21 during a field exercise where me and my platoon spent about a week out in the woods, not eating or drinking too much. When we returned to civilization on a Friday, I was ready to party. Fucking 21! My friends on the other hand, not so much. They were much more intelligent than me and told me that we should get a good night sleep, eat some food, drink some water, and we would go out the following night. I didn't want to hear it. With dirt in my ears and camouflage paint on my face, I went to the store and picked up my first 12 pack of beer. Bud Select. I returned to my barracks and started drinking and I finally convinced one guy to go out with me. We went out to Texas Roadhouse where I ordered my first beer. We ate and I thought the night was coming to an end when just then, my platoon walked in saying they couldn't leave me alone on my 21st. YESSS! They took me to a local dive bar where the bartender was getting a kick out of feeding the newly 21-year-old shots. At this point, I blacked out. The next part of the story is as told by my friends. They saw me strike up a conversation with two women. We were laughing and giggling (wish sober me was this good). Eventually, they saw me leave with these two women and they assumed I was on my way to christen my new manhood. Back to me. I wake up in the backseat of a moving car to the sound of a strange woman asking me where I live. I assess the situation and realize that I am in a town about an hour away from where I should be. Again she asks where I live. I ask her what I'm doing in this strange town and she replies that she is taking me home.

Apparently, in my blacked-out state, I told her I was a college student at a nearby college and she was being kind and taking me home. (It was not cool to be military in a military town so no doubt I was trying to impress her) Confused, I told her I was military and lived back the other way and she needs to take me back there. As you can imagine... this did not sit well with her and her friend. After some choice words, she pulled over at a gas station and "escorted" me out of the vehicle. It is now 3am, I'm an hour away from home, and I'm sitting outside a gas station. This is before Uber so I began to call every contact in my phone. EVERY CONTACT. Finally, one guy answered and just so happen to not be that far away. He agreed to pick me up and I slept on his girlfriend's bean bag chair that night. In the morning, he took me back to the barracks where I passed out from dehydration and malnourishment. My Doc had to pump two IV bags into me and told me I almost died. That is how my 21st Birthday almost killed me.

DIPPING MY TOE IN THE WATER

These early years freshly out of high school and out on my own were awkward times. A lot of new life experiences. A lot of new people. One of these new experiences was getting into a bar for the first time. I was underage, but I knew the bouncer, so I was able to get into my first bar at age 19. I felt like I was in a fantasy land. All these attractive women, nice décor, and nice drinks. It was a far cry from the barn parties and barracks room nights I was accustomed to at this point in my life. The friend I was with was much more outgoing than I was, and he was able to strike up a conversation with two women. Looking back now, I have no clue why these women would talk to us. We were both 19ish and looked about 16. We had weird high and tight haircuts and clothes that we found on the discount rack at Goodwill. But there we are. After a bit, I wanted to impress my newly found date. I remember asking myself what people do in this situation? Buy her a shot of course! I ask her what she wants, and she says, "Whatever you want." I have no idea what I want. This is my first time ordering a shot. The one liquor I could think of was Jack Daniels. I got to the bar and was thinking I really wanted to show her how manly I am, so I ordered two double-shots of Jack Daniels straight. The bartender even looked at me for an extra second, questioning my order. He pours the drinks and hands me the tab. I do not remember what it was, I do remember thinking to myself how anyone affords to come out to bars. I take my first shots ever ordered over to my date and hand over her shot. She asks what it is and with a slight grin on my face, I reply with "My favorite shot." (It wasn't) She takes that double-shot down like a champ. Not even a squinty face. I knew I had to match her confidence and down mine. I immediately start to feel my mouth watering and knew what was about to happen, but it was too late to stop. I threw up all over this girl's shoe. I now had the attention of the entire bar and all I could do is just throw up the remaining liquid in my stomach. The same bouncer that was nice enough to let me in was now the guy escorting me out. I did not get her phone number.

INTERNATIONAL FAILURE

The military did offer me the chance to travel the World. On one of these trips, I found myself in a country called Malta. We were allowed to go out and about for two days. Of course, me and my friends travel to the nearest bar which was just around the corner on the beach. There, we ran into a group of local Maltese girls and struck up a conversation. In my experience, whenever my group of friends strikes up conversation with a group of girlfriends, I know to just go for the ugliest girl in the group. 1) They are the easiest to talk to. 2) I don't have to compete with my better-looking friends. So relying on past experience, I talk to the ugliest girl in the group. After a few drinks and laughs, we all decide to separate and come back together for some night drinking and shenanigans. The girls said they wanted to meet up at midnight, which seemed really late to us. This is because we are stupid and did not realize that bars there are open until sunrise. Going off this stupidity, we decide we will go out early around 10pm and pregame. Genius. We begin doing shots and waiting on the girls. They do show up around midnight and I continue talking to my ugly girl. (A little prettier now) After about an hour or so, her friend comes over and she is jarringly taken away. I was confused but didn't think much of it and continued to sit and drink my beer. A few minutes later they both return and stand right in front of me. The friend states that earlier in the day, she "called dibs" on me to her friends, but I did not seem interested because I kept talking to the ugly friend. I was shocked. Two girls fighting over me? Is this the greatest country ever? Do I really love America? What is the penalty if I don't leave with the military? All valid questions at this point of the night. The friend stated that I must choose one of them. What a conundrum. On one hand you have the smart, witty, funny ugly girl you have been talking to all night. On the other hand, you have the hot girl. I chose the hot girl. It would all be for naught though. Because of our decision to pregame at 10pm, I was not prepared for the night. I ended up getting too drunk and passed out on the beach around 3am. I still think about those girls from time to time.... I wonder if they think of me.

THREESOME

My military career was coming to an end. Before I could get out though, I had to embarrass myself one or two more times. One day, my barracks roommate came in saying he had good news. His girlfriend from back home was coming to visit and she was bringing two friends. TWO. I mean, one of them has to like me right? These girls show up to the barracks and in traditional kid fashion, we start drinking. We obviously did not do any prior planning because 11pm came around and we realized that we were not allowed to have girls spend the night in the barracks. We got in the car and drove to the nearest (and cheapest) motel we could find. We got a room and headed up. My friend and his girlfriend immediately hopped on one of the two beds and start going at it. I mean really going at it. Legs and arms just poking out of the blankets everywhere. I head into the bathroom for a second. My bed was right outside the bathroom door and the other two girls were sitting on the bed talking. The door was basically paper so I was able to hear what they were saying. One girl says "I'll fuck him first, and then you can fuck him." The other replies "That sounds good to me". WHAT?! This is what guys dream of. It's happening. After a quick pep talk with my penis, I zip up and head out to the bed. I lay in the middle and one girl is on my right, and the other is on my left. I start kissing one and the other begins to go downtown. After about thirty seconds of some work downtown, I noticed there was no movement. Not only was there no movement, I think my penis actually began to shrivel up inside of itself. Now I'm thinking about it making matters worse. The poor girl downtown gets up and says "I have to go to the bathroom." and her friend on my right joins her. As I said earlier, you can clearly hear what happens on the other side of the door. One girl asks "What's wrong with him?" and the other offers the theory of "Maybe he's gay". After a quick look across the room at karma sutra act being conducted by my friend, I try to get matters going on my own, but no luck. The girls come out of the bathroom and one sleeps on the floor while the other moves as far away from me as possible on the bed like I was a leper. After no sleep, me and my roommate had to get up and go back to the barracks. In the hotel hallway, he high fives me and says how pumped he is that I got two girls last night! I was in a dilemma. Do I tell him what happened or let him think I had just rocked two girl's world? Figuring he was going to find out from his girlfriend, I spilled the beans. I asked him to not tell anyone in the platoon and he agreed. By the time I went to my room, changed, and headed out to a formation, the entire platoon learned of my failure and that's how I earned the nick name "Whiskey Jay".

WITH FRIENDS LIKE THESE

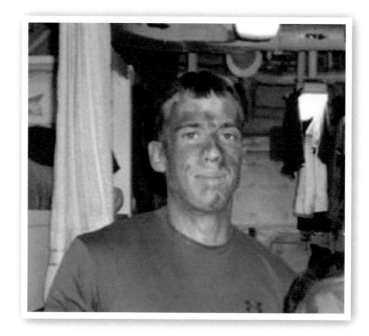

I was growing up and had a little money in my pocket right before I ended my enlistment. I used some of that money to buy a motorcycle because I'm a smart investor. Taking that bike out and about one day, I stopped and had some lunch. Apparently whatever God you believe in was smiling on me that day because this attractive girl came over and started to talking to me. She told me she was here from Australia working as a nanny and attending college. She suggested that I get a friend and she will get a friend and we all go out that night. I could not wait to get back to the barracks and share the news with my best friend. We were both excited that we had dates and we put on our best button up shirts and gel in our high and tight haircuts. We headed out to the bar where I saw Australian girl looking as beautiful as ever... her friend not so much. But what did I care? My girl was a smoke show. Sorry about your luck best friend. We sat at a table and started getting drinks having a good ol time. An hour or so into the night, I ask the table if they need any drinks and get their orders.

I walk up to the bar and wait my turn to be waited on. I suddenly feel a hand on my shoulder and it's my friend. He says, "Hey man. I just want you to know that your girl wants to fuck me. I just wanted to make sure that was cool with you." Heartbreak. He follows it with "Can I borrow your keys?". I hand over my keys and continue to wait for the drinks. I finally get the drinks and head back to the table where all that awaits now is the "not so much" girl that was Australian girl's friend. We forced conversation for a solid 10 minutes until the other two members of our party returned and then we left. I am still really good friends with that guy, but I never let him forget he owes me.

MONUMENTAL FAILURE

My military time had come to an end and I was ready to start my next endeavor. To celebrate, my friends took me to a party island in Lake Erie called Put-In-Bay. Put-In-Bay is like Las Vegas in the fact the people's inhibitions really go to the wayside. This was on full display when we were at a bar and this random girl started talking to me and within 10 minutes, she was asking where we can go to seal the deal. At that point, I was staying on my friend's boat and knew that I could not bring her back there for the sheer ridicule that I would have received from my friends. The girl was not the most attractive girl that I have ever seen. Using my quick wit, I see toward one end of the island, a **national monument**. (See what I did there?) There is no one over there at 2am right? I lead her that way. We go to the other side of the monument and lay down. She attacks me like a rabid dog that has not eaten in days.

A few seconds in, I hear some nearby bushes rustling. I try to leash the dog on top of me and tell her to calm down. I begin using my elite military training to listen to the noises while she keeps stating it was the wind and tries to nibble my ear. Just then, BAM! A huge spotlight hits us. Apparently, we were not the only drunk people ever on the island to think using the monument for a motel was a good idea. The cops had set up a minor sting operation there, but one of them slipped in the bushes which saved me from getting caught red handed. I just told the cops we were enjoying the monument and the island. They begrudgingly let us go. Phew! Undeterred, the girl I was with was still asking where to go. I was pretty much done for the night, so I took her into a bar, said I had to go to the bathroom, and left.

QUIZ EDITION: GUESS HOW THE STORY ENDS!

At this point in our journey, I'm sure you have gained some idea of how my dating life has gone. We can now use that knowledge to guess how this story ends.

I was living in Ohio for college when a friend of mine got a great idea to ride our motorcycles to the beach for the weekend. He said he knew some girls on the way we would be able to go out with for a night. Just excited to be able to talk to a girl, I was in. We began riding and stopped at the girl's house to get cleaned up before our night out on the town. We went to dinner and then out for some drinks after. Everything was going well. On the way back to her house, the girls go off on their own for "girl talk". Of course, me and my friend are congratulating ourselves on how smooth we are and how good of an idea this was. We got back to her place and that is where the night shifted. Instead of having a night cap and cuddling and watching TV or something, the girls just state that they are going to bed. She lived in a studio home, so it was all one room with two twin beds, a couch, and a loveseat. Me and my friend were confused and wondered if we did anything wrong, but she assigned sleeping arrangements and we were off to sleep. I took the couch, my date had the love seat, my friend had one bed, and his date had the other bed.

How does the story end?

A. My friend's date tries to hit on me in the middle of the night causing a girl fight over me.

B. My date moves to bed with my friend.

C. My friend has both girls while I must listen.

D. My date comes to my couch and we cuddle and talk about her ex

Answer on the last page.

THE BEST FIRST DATE I HAVE EVER BEEN ON

At this point in my life, most of my friends had wives and I was still on dating apps hoping to get a girl to reply. In a plea of desperation, I engaged my friends to find me a girl. They set me up with a girl and we arranged to go on a date. The initial conversations with her were easy. Could this be it? Could this be the girl? This girl had some connections at the local hockey rink, so we were able to get rink-side seats to watch a hockey game. It just so happens to be "dollar beer night" in the stadium also and we took full advantage. By the end of the game, we had the entire section chanting one players name on the opposing team and taunting him. "Benooooooiiiittttt" We ended up getting pictures with him and a couple of the other players. Another fan in the section wanted pictures with us too because we were apparently the first drunk couple at a sporting event she has seen. The night was going so well that we did not want it to end. I took her to the bar that I was working at and got us an entire bottle of vodka. I will repeat that. An entire bottle of vodka. It was still early on a Wednesday, so we were the only ones in the entire place drinking this bottle of vodka with the wait staff. Once the last shot was taken, it was time to head home. My apartment was within walking distance, but we just had to cut through an alleyway. In that alleyway, all the decisions I had made that night came back to haunt me. The beer at the game, the hot dog dinner, and the bottle of vodka we just drank splashed around in my stomach. I dashed behind a dumpster and those decisions came out. She was laughing so hard at me and my misfortune, that she ended up peeing her pants. That alleyway was the foundation for the longest relationship of my life. Eleven months.

THE WORST FIRST DATE I HAVE EVER BEEN ON

I have been on quite a few first dates in my life. I wish I could skip to the drooling on each other on the couch phase of a relationship, but apparently people want to get to know you before they let you drool on them. That fact leads to the first date. One particular date stands out in my mind as the worst. I was in college working at a bar to pay for my drinking habits and I met this girl as one of my customers. She showed an interest in me right off and gave me her phone number. That's a good start. We chit chatted over the next couple days and finally met up for a dinner date. I actually thought the date was going really well. I made sure to do some push ups before the date so I was looking a little bigger, I ironed my shirt, and I had a couple beers beforehand so I could kill those first date jitters. We had a nice dinner where we were laughing and drinking. I wanted to keep going. We decided to go down the street to another local bar. We sit at the bar and order drinks. Before our drinks arrive, she tells me that she sees her friend across the bar and she's going to go say hi. No problem. She gets up and begins talking to her female friend. Shortly after two guys come up to the couple of girls and strike up a conversation. I don't think much of it because this girl is having such a good time with me and I'm sure she's just hooking up her friend. Five minutes go by. Ten minutes go by and she begins to make her way back around the bar to me. Ok, here we go. Back on the date. Let's finish strong. So I thought. She came around the bar, without saying a word to me she grabbed her beer that I had ordered for me and walked back to the other group. I was befuddled. What just happened? By the time I finished my beer I ordered, I saw the newly formed group leaving the bar together. I never got an answer on what happened that day, but I'm assuming it was she was just so overwhelmed with how attractive I was that she couldn't take it anymore.

Answer: A

Printed in the United States
By Bookmasters